OVERCOMING

ANXIETY

A Practical CBT Workbook To Ease Worry And Regain Peace.

Jennifer Smith Counsellor

Foreword

Anxiety can feel like an overwhelming force, making even the smallest moments feel exhausting. If you've ever wished for a simple, practical way to understand and manage anxiety, this workbook is for you.

This is not a book filled with complex jargon or long-winded explanations. Instead, it's designed to be easy to use, offering clear, step-by-step Cognitive Behavioural Therapy (CBT) techniques that anyone can apply. CBT is an evidence-based approach that helps people recognise and change unhelpful thought patterns, making anxiety more manageable. This workbook breaks it down in a way that feels accessible and practical—no prior knowledge of CBT is needed.

You might be using this workbook on your own as a first step toward understanding anxiety, or alongside counselling as part of your journey. Some people find that working through these exercises helps them decide whether counselling might be beneficial, while others use it as an extra tool to support therapy. Counselling can provide a safe space to explore the root causes of anxiety and develop coping strategies, while medication can be an option for those needing additional support. Everyone's path is different, and there is no right or wrong way to approach healing.

As a counsellor with many years of experience, I've used these worksheets with clients who have struggled with anxiety in various forms. They are tried and tested, offering a structured way to challenge anxious thoughts, manage physical symptoms, and regain a sense of control.

My hope is that this book empowers you to take meaningful steps toward feeling calmer, more in control, and more at peace with yourself. You are not alone in this, and change is possible.

Let's begin.

~Jenni Smith, Counsellor

Table of Contents

Introduction

Anxiety can feel overwhelming, persistent, and all-encompassing.

If you've picked up this book, you might feel like you're living in a constant state of worry unable to relax, unable to feel at peace, and always concerned about the "what-ifs" of life. This book was written with you in mind. As a therapist, I've seen how anxiety can take hold, making everyday situations feel overwhelming and leaving you exhausted by the weight of constant concern.. Whether your worries revolve around work, relationships health or the future, anxiety can make it difficult to trust yourself, feel in control, or simply enjoy the present moment. The purpose of this book is to help you manage that anxiety. By using Cognitive Behavioural Therapy (CBT) techniques, you'll learn how to identify the thought patterns fuelling your worry, challenge unhelpful beliefs, and create healthier ways to cope. You'll discover tools to manage the physical and emotional sensations of anxiety and strategies to focus on what you can control while letting go of what you can't.

This is not about "stopping" your worry altogether after all anxiety is a natural part of life. Instead it is about finding balance. It's about learning to navigate uncertainty without being consumed by it and how to shift your focus from fear to resilience. By working through this book, you'll gain insights, practical tools, and a renewed sense of calm. My hope is that it will empower you to find peace in the present, more grounded, more in control. You're not alone in this, and you're capable of change. Let's begin this journey together.

Understanding Anxiety

Anxiety is a natural response to perceived threats. It's your body's way of preparing you to face challenges or danger a system that has evolved to keep you safe. However, when this system becomes overly sensitive or constantly activated, it can feel like you're stuck in a loop of worry and tension, even when no immediate danger exists.

Anxiety often manifests in three interconnected ways:

1. **Physical Symptoms:** Racing heart, shallow breathing, muscle tension, and restlessness. These are your body's "fight, flight, or freeze" responses kicking in.

2. **Thought Patterns:** Persistent worries, imagining worst-case scenarios, or focusing on "what-ifs."

3. **Behavioural Reactions:** Avoiding certain situations, seeking constant reassurance, or trying to control things beyond your influence.

When you're anxious, these three elements reinforce one another. For example, worrying about your family may cause physical tension, which in turn heightens your anxious thoughts, creating a cycle that feels hard to break.

How Anxiety Works

At its core, anxiety is fuelled by a belief that something bad will happen and that you won't be able to cope with it. This belief triggers an alarm in your brain, sending a cascade of physical, emotional, and cognitive responses. The more you engage with these anxious thoughts and behaviours, the stronger the anxiety becomes.

How CBT Can Help

Cognitive Behavioural Therapy (CBT) is a practical, evidence-based approach that helps you understand and change the patterns keeping anxiety alive. It focuses on:

1. **Identifying Unhelpful Thoughts:** Recognise the distorted or irrational thoughts that fuel anxiety (e.g., "If I'm not constantly worrying, something bad will happen to my children").

2. **Challenging and Reframing Thoughts:** Question these thoughts and replace them with more balanced, realistic ones.

3. **Changing Behaviours:** Engage in healthier coping strategies, like addressing avoidant behaviours or practicing relaxation techniques.

4. **Breaking the Cycle:** By changing how you think and act, you reduce physical symptoms

and rewire your brain to respond differently to anxiety.

1. Triggers and Patterns: Understanding Your Anxiety

Anxiety often feels unpredictable, but it's rarely random. It's triggered by specific situations, thoughts, or events. Understanding these triggers and patterns is a critical first step in gaining control over your anxiety.

What are Triggers?

Triggers are situations, thoughts, or experiences that activate your anxiety. For example, Imagine you send an important message and don't get a reply. Your mind starts racing with worst-case scenarios Did something go wrong? Did I say the wrong thing? Anxiety thrives on uncertainty, making it easy to assume the worst even when there's no real evidence."

Identifying Patterns

Anxiety doesn't just happen it follows a pattern. Maybe it starts with a "what if" thought ("What if something bad happens?"), then escalates into imagining worst-case scenarios. Recognising these patterns can help you intervene before they spiral out of control.

Worksheet: Anxiety Triggers Journal

Purpose: Track and understand the situations, thoughts, and physical sensations that trigger your anxiety.

How to Use:

- Write a short description of the situation in the "Situation" column.
- Record the thoughts and physical sensations you experienced.
- Use the "Actions Taken" column to jot down how you responded.
- Review weekly to identify patterns.

Date/Time	Situation	Thoughts	Physical sensations	Actions Taken	Review weekly

Reflection Questions:

- Do certain themes or fears show up repeatedly?

_____

_____

_____

_____

_____

- Are there patterns with time of day or interactions?

_____

_____

_____

_____

_____

2. Challenging Anxious Thoughts

Our thoughts shape our feelings and behaviours. When we're anxious, our thoughts often become distorted, making us overestimate threats and underestimate our ability to cope.

Common Cognitive Distortions

- Catastrophising: Imagining the worst-case scenario (e.g., "If my child doesn't call, something awful has happened").
- Black-and-White Thinking: Viewing situations as all good or all bad.
- Mind Reading: Assuming you know others' thoughts (e.g., "They think I'm a terrible parent").

Steps to Challenge Anxious Thoughts

1. **Identify the Thought:** Pinpoint the exact worry causing anxiety.

2. **Examine the Evidence:** Ask, "What evidence do I have that supports or contradicts this thought?"

3. **Create a Balanced Thought:** Replace the anxious thought with a kinder, more realistic one.

Worksheet: Thought Record

Purpose: Practice identifying, challenging, and reframing unhelpful thoughts.

How to Use:

- Whenever anxiety arises, fill in each column.
- Weigh evidence for and against your thought.
- Form a balanced thought, then note emotional changes.

Date/Time	Trigger	Auto Thought	Evidence Positive or negative	Balanced Thought	New Feeling

3. Calming the Body: Managing Physical Symptoms

Anxiety manifests in the body through symptoms like racing heart, tense muscles, and shallow breathing. Calming your body is a key part of managing anxiety.

Understanding the Stress Response

The "fight or flight" response helps in emergencies but drains you when activated too frequently.

Strategies to Calm the Body

- **Deep Breathing:** Inhale for four, hold for four, exhale for six.
- **Progressive Muscle Relaxation:** Tense and relax each muscle group.
- **Grounding Exercises:** Identify sensory details (5 things you see, 4 you can touch, etc.).
- **Physical Activity:** Burn off stress hormones through movement.

Worksheet: Body Awareness & Relaxation Log

Purpose: Observe bodily cues and record which relaxation methods help.

How to Use:

- Note physical sensations when you feel anxious.
- Record which technique you tried and rate its effectiveness.
- Consider how you might improve or combine techniques.

Date/Time	Physical Sensations	Technique Used	Effectiveness (1-10)	Notes/Next Steps

4. Focusing on What You Can Control

Anxiety often stems from trying to control what you can't. Sorting out what's within your control can help direct your energy wisely.

Worksheet: Control & Influence Map

Purpose: Visually organise your worries based on control, influence, or acceptance.

How to Use:

1. Draw three circles like a target.
2. Label the centre "Control," the middle "Influence," and the outer ring "No Control."
3. Write your worries in the appropriate circle.

Worry Circle (Control, Influence, No Control) Actions to Take

Reflection Questions:

- How can you focus on the circles you truly control or influence?

_____

_____

_____

_____

_____

- Can you practice acceptance for what lies outside your control?

_____

_____

_____

_____

_____

5. Building Self-Compassion

Self-compassion means extending the kindness to yourself that you'd show a close friend.

Why Self-Compassion Matters

Studies show self-compassion reduces anxiety and increases resilience. Recognising everyone has struggles frees you from perfectionism and guilt.

Worksheet: Self-Compassion Reflections

Purpose: Shift from self-criticism to self-kindness.

How to Use:

1. Recall a recent situation where you felt anxious or guilty.
2. Write what you would say to a friend in the same situation.
3. List three self-care actions you can do today.
4. Reflect on how self-compassion might change your perspective.

Situation Self-Compassionate Statement Self-Care
Actions

Reflection Questions:

- How do you feel after practicing self-compassion?

_____

_____

_____

_____

_____

- What changes when you treat yourself kindly?

_____

_____

_____

_____

_____

6. Practicing Mindfulness

Mindfulness involves staying present and non-judgmental. It helps break the cycle of "what-if" thinking and anchors you in the here and now.

Simple Mindfulness Techniques

- **Breath Awareness:** Notice each inhale and exhale.
- **Body Scan:** Check for tension from feet to head.
- **Mindful Observing:** Examine an object's details in the moment.

Purpose: Track and reflect on daily mindfulness exercises.

How to Use:

- Choose a mindfulness technique.
- Practice for at least 5 minutes daily.

Reflect on how it affects your mood.

Worksheet: Daily Mindfulness Practice

Day	Technique Used	Minutes Practiced	Mood Before	Mood After	Notes/ Insights
Monday					
Tuesday					
Wednesday					
Thursday					
Friday					
Saturday					
Sunday					

Reflection Questions:

- Do you notice a difference in your overall anxiety levels after practicing mindfulness?

_____

_____

_____

_____

_____

- Which techniques work best for you?

_____

_____

_____

_____

_____

7. Creating a Personal Action Plan

A personal action plan helps you pull together all the tools and ideas you've gathered.

Components of Your Plan

1. Identify Triggers
2. Go-To Strategies
3. Support System
4. Daily Routines
5. Reflection and Adjustment

Worksheet: My Anxiety Action Plan

Purpose: Outline a plan to use when anxious thoughts arise.

Trigger	Strategy/ Technique	Support Person	Routine/Hab it	Notes/ Adjustments

Reflection Questions:

- Are there any strategies you'd like to add to your plan?

_____

_____

_____

_____

_____

- How can you make your plan easier to follow?

_____

_____

_____

_____

_____

8. Sustaining Change

Progress in managing anxiety is a big step, but maintaining it can be just as challenging. Life is unpredictable, and anxiety can resurface.

Anticipating Setbacks

Setbacks happen in any change process. View them as opportunities:

- What triggered this setback?
- Which coping skills might help?
- What can you learn from this experience?

Staying Accountable

- **Regular Check-Ins:** Weekly or monthly reviews.
- **Journaling:** Track triggers, worries, and successes.
- **Buddy System:** Share progress with a friend who understands.

Refreshing Your Skills

- Re-read relevant sections.

- Update worksheets when things change.

- Seek Professional Support if you feel stuck.

Conclusion: Words of Encouragement & Summary of the Journey

You've now explored:

- **Anxiety Patterns:** How it manifests in thoughts, body, and behaviours.
- **Challenging Thoughts:** Transforming anxious beliefs into balanced perspectives.
- **Body Calming:** Techniques like deep breathing and muscle relaxation.
- **Control vs. Letting Go:** Focusing on what's truly within your influence.
- **Self-Compassion:** Treating yourself with the kindness you'd show a friend.
- **Mindfulness:** Anchoring your awareness in the present moment.
- **Personal Action Plan:** Mapping out strategies and support networks.

- **Sustaining Change:** Embracing setbacks as part of growth.

A Final Note

Change often unfolds in small, consistent steps. You have the tools to pause, reflect, and choose healthier responses to anxiety. Keep practicing and adapting these techniques as life evolves.

Each time you choose awareness over worry, acceptance over control, and kindness over self-criticism, you strengthen your capacity for calm and resilience.

You've come this far keep going. Trust in your ability to navigate uncertainty and remain connected to the calm, caring presence within. Here to your continued growth and well-being!

Printed in Great Britain
by Amazon